Threkjshanelle

Collection Seven

Threkjshanelle

◆

Collection Seven

Jonathan Christopher Martin

Writers Club Press
New York Lincoln Shanghai

Threkjshanelle
Collection Seven

Writers Club Press
an imprint of iUniverse, Inc.

For information address:
iUniverse
2021 Pine Lake Road, Suite 100
Lincoln, NE 68512
www.iuniverse.com

ISBN: 0-595-26349-6

Printed in the United States of America

Dedication

◆

All my love to my sister Sherri, my children, my mothers, Aunt Ruby, Mary, Tim, Cathy, Jim, Mike, Kendall, Paul, and Lisa.

Special thanks to God. You held me together throughout this chaos…This sadness

Epigraph

◆

I still have myself, I still have me…

Table of Contents

◆

Preface

◆

Threkjshanelle

It's dark in here you know…In my mind, in my heart. I used to be a knight in shining armor. As of late my armor has gone rusty and my gallantry, it seems, has been for not all these years.

Is there no light in this world? Can there be no peace within me?

Have you ever just wanted to take time for *you*? To have one day that was all yours, to do what you wanted, where you wanted, when you wanted? Take a walk, go shopping and buy something only you could appreciate, or maybe even to be in love for a day.

I am finding myself appreciating the little things in life more and more each day. I also find my regrets piling up as well. The "would have-should have-could haves" of my past tense haunt me.

If only true love, were true.

—*Jonathan Christopher Martin*
October 13, 2002

x

Acknowledgements

◆

Cover model: Lisa Priest as Elisa Jayne Priest
from the upcoming threkjshanelle,
Tainted: Threkjshanelle Collection Nine

Introduction

◆

You may ask me, why seven? Why now?

My answer: SEPTEMBER…THE END

Of Milk & Blisters

◆

Nuclear Winter

◆

White with despair
Is my blackened heart

A traitor to me
I've become, in part

An anger that snows
Burns ice through my veins

Do you miss me?

A shadow that whispers
It whispers my name

Then swallows me up
And snuffs out my flame

An anger that snows
Burns ice through my veins

Do you wish me? Dead…

KeliAnna

◆

Everyone wants you
To capture your perfection

To catch the earthbound angel
And hold on tightly

No flaws they see in you
Just a heart so warm, so true

But little can they see
How you burn

For a love as true as you are

Someday My Day Will Come

◆

Dreams are torn
Then plowed under
Of sad times born
Made so simple
Feeding on the pangs of nevermore

Wishes fade
They are nothing
But a loving
Memory
Feeding on the pangs of nevermore

Someday my day will come
(Someday my day will come)

And when it does, I'm gonna love it

Someday my day will come
(Someday my day will come)

And when it does, tears fall like rain

There is joy in me again…

Lost you on
A day so tragic
Never will I
Be the same
Bleeding from my eyes forevermore

Time won't heal
The wound you left here
In this empty
Space I fill
Bleeding from my eyes forevermore

Someday my day will come
(Someday my day will come)

And when it does, I'm gonna love it

Someday my day will come
(Someday my day will come)

And when it does, tears fall like rain

There is peace in me again…

Someday my day will come
(Someday my day will come)

And when it does, I'm gonna love it
(Someday my day will come)

Someday my day will come
(Someday my day will come)

And when it does, tears fall like rain

And wash away, all the pain…

Lament

◆

This world not made
For such as we

Our kind, who feel so deeply
Our kind, who feed on longing

Never shall your love bare fruit
Not with one so shallow

If ever paths do cross in time
I shall be yours, you shall be mine

Open Wound

◆

My love for you,
An open wound

Will you mend it
Make it better

Or salt it
And bring me madness

The End

◆

Didn't think it could come to this
Couldn't know it would hurt so bad

No longer touch, no longer kiss
No longer anything of what we had

Holding on like leaves in an autumn wind
Then comes the fall, we spiral down

As I felt the clouds set in
I knew that I would surely drown
In a pool of contempt

Lisa-Jayne

◆

Angel

◆

You resurrect feelings long since dead
I cry the tears of yesterdays shed

My heart's ragged fabric
Stained well with sorrow

My eyes so hollow
Staring at she who fills them

Un-Promise

♦

This throwaway love
As it seems
Nothing's for real
Nothing is real

Opened my heart
You threw it away
Nothing's for real
Nothing is real

Your words to me, so sweet
Now bittersweet
How I fell for all your lies

Once thought you true, to me
But not, I see
I found your truth was in disguise

This throwaway dream
As it were

Nothing's for real
Nothing is real

Opened my arms
You cast them aside
Nothing's for real
Nothing is real

I bled tears for you
But now I'm through
I walk away from all your lies

A stronger me
I live to see
Wiping dark days for my eyes

You will never,
You will never,
Find another love like me

You will never,
You will never,
Find me shedding tears for thee

Again…

For Elise

◆

The first day I saw you
Was the first day
Of the rest of my life

As I touched your silken lips
My breath quickened
I could not catch it

When I heard your name
Upon the wind
I turned to see you

Standing in love's shadow

Paravax No. 3876

◆

You are,
Like no other

I can't recall your name
Stare at me in wonder as

I am.

Paramour de Taos

◆

She calls to me
My Navajo princess
Hair of blackened silk
And eyes so dark with mystery

No other can replace her
In my heart, or in my thoughts

As turquoise skies fade to onyx hues
Our shadows bleed together

As fires of the night

Til I See You Again

◆

I am saddened unto my depths
Taken from me without a kiss

You were this day

Love is such a simple word
The way I feel goes beyond it

Fate is my punishment

Someday,
Someway,
I will fold into your arms

The Nothing That Never Dies

———————— ◆ ————————

Lonely is a dragon
I cannot slay

It is a glass
Never filled

It is a rotting state
It is decay

A nagging voice,
Never stilled

Lonely is an open sore
It is the banshee's forlorn cries

Lonely is a bitter tea
It is the nothing that never dies

Tuesday

◆

Tiny drops dot my window
I look out onto the gray afternoon
Waiting to be with you
Waiting for it to be you

Warm away rough edges
Gaze into the fire
Knowing that I too burn for you

I watch you, thanking God
For each and every day

With you

Dreaming

◆

When I wake,
I dream of you

As I sleep,
You are here

Capricorn Eyes

◆

Mes Enfants Précieux

◆

Noble girl
Apple of my eye
Tell me your hopes and dreams
Anytime you feel unsure
Simply ask me, I will tell
How much I love you
Always will

Ketchup smeared on kitten cheeks
Always into everything
Teddy bears and chewing gum
Your favorites any day
Jumping, dancing, having fun
And stealing my heart along the way

Just when I thought my heart was full
Of love from two
Rellian third come bring your light
Even now I burst with joy
The son is shining, all around the world…

Broken Destiny

♦

I've sought you for a thousand years
Never finding, always hoping
For a love so true
A heart so pure

Making no sense of this world

False kisses, fake embraces
Lies on top of lies
Is what I found
And how I lived

Til came you

As irony is quite ironic
As fate is often fatal
I bare no shock
My life is tainted

I find my destiny, now broken

Will you be swiftly taken
Away forever, away to never
See how much is here
Within me

Or shall I find you once again

Where destinies lie unbroken

Bones Slip Satin

◆

Rude Awakening

◆

All these years asleep
While eyes were shut wide open

Never known to keep
A tainted view in hoping

That somehow, someday
You'd come back to me and say

"I'm sorry…"

Forbidden

◆

We are bound
Broken, yet unbroken

We two hearts

There is a promise
Left unspoken

For we cannot be

Yet we be…

Rot-hole Bookstore

◆

Could I ever know such arrogance
Here in my own hometown
I came to love you as a boy
Never thought to be scorned by you as a man
On far away days
Often did I travel to other lands, other times
Keeping treasures in my mind

But now that I am captain
Of vessels, with words as sails
Only hoping I too, could bring such pleasure
Kings and queens of ignorance
Steal my dreams
Take my ambition from me
Only for the moment
Realize this…
Every day I get stronger

You will see me elsewhere
On a self
Underestimate me if you dare

Someday you will crawl
Underneath yourselves
Contemplating your obtuse treatment
Knowing you once spat on me

Rusty Nails

Beloved Skank

My throat is dry
My throat is sore

I would call you slut
I would call you whore

But I can't, you see
I love you still

No matter what you've done to me,
I will

Layoff

———— ◆ ————

Rest in pieces my old friend,
Never thought that it would end

Vaseline? It will be missed
Bend you over, not even kissed

How's the wife?
How's the kids?

How is life
In the skids?

You poor bloody sod…

Gizzard Twist

◆

Lick your eyeballs
Gizzard Twist

Eat brain matter
From the ceiling

Flex your nostrils
Gizzard Twist

Rare perfume
That's so appealing

I don't need anyone to tell me
Who to date
Or who to mate with

I don't need anyone to show me
Who is great
Or greatly thought of

Wash those dishes
Gizzard Twist

Forks and spoons and knives
Adore you

Mash your veggies
Gizzard Twist

Spitting acid,
Walking proudly.

Hairy Little Catfish

♦

In my pocket
A ball of lint

Hairy little catfish
Came and went

In old buckets
Gills and fins

Hairy little catfish
Back again

Eat Your Veggies

◆

Eat your veggies little brat
Or your head shall never grow

Big enough to fill a hat
Or read a book of Poe

Drink your milk, you little sod
To be one day so tall

Drink it now, don't just nod
Or all your teeth will fall

Stripjoint

◆

Women! Women!
Everywhere
And not a drop to drink

Some are tall
Some are short
Some will make you think

Slap a dollar on the table
Watch her bob about
Steal some kisses if yer able
Before they throw you out

Roadkill

◆

Compact vittles
On the street

Turning colors
From the heat

As a snack
Or as a meal

Grub all day
Such a deal!

Angelo

◆

Mack Daddy king
Pimp Dragon prince

As your tongue wags
You make women wince

Are you for real
Or just a tease

Put new victims
To their knees

A Child Is Crying

◆

A child is crying
In the storm

For loving comfort
Safe from harm

Little one wanting
Happiness without strings

Of milk, of cookies
And bedtime things

A teddy to hug
A goodnight kiss
A happily ever after
This…

Tainted Lover

◆

You try and make peace
With my mouth

Never sure
What this is

Nervous pimples bead my skin
Your heart intimidates me
Your heart intimidates me

You try to raise me
From my death

Never sure
What this is

Told no lies, only truth
Yet your breath impales me
Yet your breath impales me

You knew it from the very start
I was another's…Not in heart
You filled my spirit, now it's black
Gave love to me, now you attack

Never sure
What this is

Never sure
What this is

You say you're sorry
As do I

Never sure
What this is

Sad water flowing as if wine
Pain drinks corruption from we
Pain drinks corruption from we

You walk away now
Void is me

Never sure
What this is

How the years have passed away
My love for you un-faded
My love for you un-faded

You knew it from the very start
I was another's, not in heart
You fill my spirit once again
Gave love to me and was my friend

Now I'm sure
What this is

Ever sure
What this is

Kissing Kessel

Mikki

◆

Your love
Waters the empty gardens of my heart

I am safe nowhere
I am whole, not at all

Unless it is in the shadow of your tender smile

You are
My sacred friend

My endless sunburst
Casting radiance on dark corners

Of this sad and dismal life

Failure

◆

All alone I stand
With no destiny at hand

Noble efforts gone to waste
If only I could steal a taste

Of everlasting love

Grandma

◆

I treasure you
For all you are

I treasure you
For all you were

In dark times
You light the way

To all the treasures of the heart

No One

◆

Never will I let you go
Over time as love grows empty

Only you can fill me
Nothing else
Ever will, ever could

Watching from afar
I see the evil
Lurking
Looming

Keep us safe and strong
Even as the storm draws near us
Even as it bares its thorns
Place your hand in mine

Understand that I am here
See my heart, it has not changed

Alone I stood against the wind
Pain my only companion

Alone no more, for you are here
Running tears from bitter eyes
Thorns and rain subside…

Leather Jacket

◆

Keep me dry and warm
My Leathers
Keep me safe from harm

Give me love as no woman will
My leathers
You won't break my heart

My leathers, my best friend

Tauni Novaana

◆

Carry me far from here
Tauni Novaana take flight

Faster and farther still
From sunrise to starry night

Sherri

◆

My dearest sister
My dearest friend

I miss you so
When miles separate

Love is not an adequate word
To describe my heart

Only God can hold
A higher meaning in my life

You are so far from me
Yet always here with me

I love you

Lover

◆

Will you, my angel
Will you lift me above
This circumstance

Can you make the sun rise
As you did when we met

I miss the tender taste
Of you

Never could I find
Someone to fill

My empty wanting

September

———————◆———————

September is a wind a change
September is a kiss of sorrow

No more "I love you's" answered with silence
No more promises for you to forsake

Endings become beginnings
In a single breath

As I tell you goodbye…

Candy Bar Kiss

◆

I like the chocolate in your kiss

Candy coated tenderness
Only you can give
Useless to pretend
Looks as though I'm trapped again
Deliciously so

Eagerly I want to taste you
As your trappings unwrap
Tell me how you got so sweet

Yours is a confection
Others cannot touch
Underneath these satin sheets

Underneath a moonlit sky
Passion rides the night

Sister Sinister

◆

Halloween

◆

Fangs enrapture
Silken napes

Bones are walking
From their graves

Young ones prowling
In theirs capes

Seeking sweets galore

Wolves at worship
Moon aglow

Warlock cast
Another spell

Creatures scamper
To and fro

Wings on high they soar

Throat Torn Open

◆

Excuse me whilst I slit my throat
And reach inside
And pull out tissue

Pardon messes made on floors
On clothes
In bathroom basins

If you should get the letter
That says
I should know better

But did not

Sing a song for me
Tell some tales of my life
Cherish my memory

Divorce Mosh

◆

Once upon a time
I was a boy

Never ever angry
No need to destroy

Then I met you
Now all that it through

I didn't think love should be like this

You started with my heart
Ripped it all apart

Now I'm very angry
Can't you see

You took my little girl
My precious little joy

Gonna make you pay for it…
Pay in full. Die!

(This gun no toy)
Die! Die! Die! Die!

(Everything destroy)
Die! Die! Die! Die!

(Your death my joy)
Die! Die! Die! Die!
Die! Die! Die! Die!

How I Hate You

◆

I hate you in the morning when I wake
I loathe you as I bed for the night
I despise your every movement

This is how I feel
This what you made of me

All your lies
All the pain you gave

Like some present
Like a gift so neatly wrapped

Thank you for this remembrance

Suicide My Bride

◆

I don't know anymore
If I will be around

To see another day
My thoughts are far from this place

I don't know who I am
And I don't even care

If I live or die
I just don't care anymore

Feel the blade
Rush across my throat

Yet I bleed no pain
Only memories

Of what I had long before
No matter, time to go

To where peace is home
No longer need this flesh

I just don't care anymore

Troll Snack

◆

Eyeballs
Eyeballs
Googly little eyeballs

Eyeballs
Eyeballs
Slurp 'em down

Ah!

Rydoc

◆

Do you know your nightmares?
Dark dreams of daylight
Rushing through your mind
Like winds on high
The reoccurring kind

Now die do I
To find my past
Secure the future
Stop the raging in my head

I live a hell
Can't break the spell
Alas my love,
I'm dead

Thorn Strewn Tinderbox

◆

Flennoy

◆

Brilliant, yet lunatic
Suave, yet ghetto-fide

You were my friend
You were my brother
You were my father-kind

Now you are gone

How have you been?
Are you dead?

Do you still breathe?
Do you still laugh?

A king be you now
Or a drunken fool

What have you become?

Beyond The Shadow

◆

Deeply sleeping in a grave
Entombed in my confusion

You spat at me, now I decay
Was our love illusion?

Beyond the shadow of a lie
I tell myself, "I want you still"

Truth be known, to watch you die
Would give me such a thrill…

Aching Emptiness

◆

Emptiness is a union of two
With only one heart beating

Emptiness is a hunger
For someone you will never taste

Aching emptiness is your love,
For it is barren

For Hate Sake

◆

For hate sake
I spit in the wine I serve you

For hate sake
I make your bride my mistress

For hate sake
I tell lies about you in the streets

For hate sake
I call you friend

Can you feel the knife at your back?

Ebony War Prince

---◆---

I am black
As the night I travel
Feel me voice against your skin

I am fire
Burning ice into your lungs
Taste the blade I twist within you

Dear enemy, dear prey
Bleed my wrath upon you

Empty Wallet

◆

God knows I try
Only to fail, only to lose
This fight to keep a dollar

No winners here
Others make it just fine

My luck done disappeared
Over yonder where I,
Never make it to
Even when I work til dead
You know I'll have no coins to lay on my eyes

Hello Me

◆

I met myself today
Was not thrilled
To say the least

Thoughts once clear
Were gray and stilled
Old bones creaked like unsteady wood

Disappointment was a shadow
Ever present, ever nagging

Time had woven
Threads of failure
Into life's tapestry

Now a ghost
I saw in me
Of who I was, and longed to be

Disappointment was a shadow
Ever present, ever nagging

Ever me...

Cocteau-ed

◆

Such music of a lifetime
Enough to save me
From myself

What angel sings to me
Liz, no other but herself

No other makes me weep

This beauty called a memory
Enough to keep me
Sweetly dreaming

Those eyes, that mouth
Liz, no other but herself

No other binds so deep

Of Basil & Circumstance

◆

Raining Inside My Heart

◆

It is raining inside myself
Regrets trickle from my eyes

Sorrow pushed sad water
From its depths

To spill upon me
To remind me

Of you

Perished

◆

Here it comes again

The madness, the struggle
Will nothing be at ease
Will no one give me peace

Why must it be so

I have loved, I have longed
Only to be slain
Only to be wasted

This darkness fills my table

Every cup is spiced with torment
I drink of you and I am poisoned
I drink of you…I am murdered

Taken

◆

Where has it gone
This brooding, this twinge

Taken,

By the gentle love
Within you

Little Prince

♦

Join this realm my little one
On this day
Rejoice
Every eye upon you
Now your time has come

Assasin

◆

Even though I know it true
Little does it reconcile
I realize "Nothing personal"
Should be the way of things
Alas to see the style of it

Presently leads one thinking that
Reward is not just pay
I saw the grin upon you
Every bullet, every blade
Soon becomes a plaything
To snatch a life away

OthersAfter

◆

Paul M. Carthart

Life's Road

◆

by Paul M. Carhart

When all is said and done
When I stand before The Throne
What will matter most?
My job? My friends? My home?

Or is it more example?
The way I treat each person
The way in which I reach out
No matter what the season

Perhaps it's partly all of this
For that's where life is found
In death we rise to heaven
Life's road is on the ground

Nothing I Have Felt

◆

by Paul M. Carhart

Nothing I have felt is unique
Yet I grant such importance
To what I think
To what I believe
To what I feel
And so I should

So, also, should you

Basia Sobieraj

Black Soul

◆

By Basia Sobieraj

I didn't dream about a white soul
I didn't have to

It seems to be that I have it
But it turned out to be un-truth

Although it was a soul
But in a different color
Its blackness flooded in me good faith

Nothing can help…

Let Us Fly

◆

By Basia Sobieraj

Have I told you lately what I feel
Have you told me lately that you care
Have our souls met each other lately somewhere here
Have they ever met…
In the place between the heaven and the earth

Let our souls search their mates
Let them fly

Let us show to the world smiling faces
And please don't deny

It is not our time,
Let us fly!

© 2002 Basia Sobieraj

Love At First Anything

◆

By Basia Sobieraj

Looking from behind lace curtains of eyelashes
Confirmed by curtains of eyelids

Lips wandered in a direction
Of smile sent to you

A palm stroked, brushed unintentionally
Open, although clenched

Suddenly trembling when you listen
A sound of a voice you will remember

This happens some,
During a first meeting

Something beautiful came our way

At first word
Sowed deep inside a soul

It ordered us to believe that
It was worthy to move even heaven and earth

Indeed, really befell us nothing more than
Love at first, anything

© 2002 Basia Sobieraj

Kevin McFarland

---◆---

The Other Side Of The Rainbow

◆

By Kevin McFarland
(for Keli)

Empty is the night
Knowing we are apart
Lonely is the silent air,
Without you to share a dream
Lost is my soul
When you're not around
Barren are the surroundings
In the absence of your being

Found have I,
The very thing that would make me breathe
Yet so far away and removed seems she,
And in yearning my heart bleeds

Oh fruitless night
Must I be tormented so?

"Yes" replies the wind, "If you would reach the pot of gold
For the other end of the rainbow
Is no easy walk
And many who start thereon
Eventually fall off
But if in spite of your aches
And the pining of thy heart
You stay true to your word
As the first step from the start,
You will get yours in the end
If she truly is that more than "special friend"

Not terribly consoling words
To one inflicted as such
Yet no choice do I have
Having already given myself so much
To the possibility of a tomorrow
And my heart already so touched

I fade off to dreaming
Though restlessly so
Knowing there'll never be a true night's rest
Until we are one entwined
In love's endearing throes

Keli Handwerk

◆

A Voice In The Night

◆

By Keli Handwerk

I can still hear the echo of your voice
The sounds of your guitar strumming softly
Only in the wind now,
That you are departed from me.

I can still see the strong man you once were
Gently smiling down at me
As I admire your strength and talents
Standing tall, your laughter surrounding me.

I can still remember the sadness in your eyes
Even though you guided me and hoped for me
There were dreams unfulfilled for you
That you could never realize.

I could sense defeat underneath you victories
As you continued down life's unpredictable path
As you met each obstacle and overcame many
But never met the goal that you had intended.

I knew there would be little that you could leave me
Except for the voice in the night
And that I will hold in my heart and cherish
As I sing the melodies that you gave me as your gift.

I can only sing your songs now as I remember
The love that only a father can give
In that way, you will still live
In my heart and in my soul as my special memory.

A voice in the night will guide me
And triumph in my accomplishments and in my life
To know that your legacy was far more treasured
Than riches or gold.
I know that you can rest now in peaceful bliss
As you give up this life with all its turmoil
Your body will be strong again
And with a solemn kiss we say "Goodbye."

© 2002 Keli Handwerk

Lisa Priest

Thoughts

───────◆───────

By Lisa Priest

Dreams and accomplishments
Are only steps away
To travel, and put your feet in the sand
On some beach far from here

Spending all your time
With someone really special
Then you will know
You have the good life

Love Is

◆

By Lisa Priest

Love is a dove
Flying high above the towers.

Love is like
A flower opening its pedals.

Love is
Being with the ones that are close to you.
Like wishing you were here with me…

Lisa Brodsky

---◆---

Chakara Darkhallows

◆

By Lisa Brodsky

The winds of pain
Fly at my back

Screams of torture
Follow my steps

The blood on my hands
Staining my world

© 2002 Lisa Brodsky

Death Is Life, Life Is Death

◆

By Lisa Brodsky

My righteous anger
My unjust love
My fitful pains

And soulful woes

A blood soaked pen
A silver tipped blade
A hangman's noose

And knots so tight

So much decay
So much loss
So much death

And prayers unheard

With ashes I see
With rage I know
With anguish I remember

And my soul I do release

Hate is not power
Hate is not evil
Hate is energy
And it is spent often

My righteous anger
A silver tipped blade
So much death

And my soul, I do release…

© 2002 Lisa Brodsky

Afterword

◆

I truly hope you enjoyed this book. I would love to hear from you.

May you walk in happiness. Always...

—*Jon*

6

Sahchee-von du' Threkjshanelle

◆

Books in the Threkjshanelle series:

Threkjshanelle Collection One

Threkjshanelle Collection Two

Threkjshanelle Collection Three

Unhappily Ever After: Threkjshanelle Collection Four

The Book of Christmas: Threkjshanelle Collection Five

Threkjshanelle Collection Six

Threkjshanelle Collection Seven

Threkjshanelle Collection Eight

Tainted: Threkjshanelle Collection Nine

The Book of Valentine: Threkjshanelle Collection Ten

All Others After: Threkjshanelle Collection Eleven

Of Body and Mind: Threkjshanelle Collection Twelve

The Book of Hatred: Threkjshanelle Collection Thirteen

Jonathan Martin can be contacted at any of the following:

jonathan.martin@usa.net
broken_fixme@hotmail.com

Jonathan Martin c/o THREKJSHANELLE
P.O. Box 62623
Colorado Springs, Colorado 80962

Paul M. Carhart is a master of modern speculative fiction. See for yourself:
www.paulcarhart.com

Lisa Priest can be contacted at:
P.O. Box 62623
Colorado Springs, Colorado 80962

After all these years I'm still Cocteau-ed. Find out what Liz Fraser is up to these days:
www.elizabethfraser.com

Dragons, wizards and bears…Oh my! What has he painted this time? What are you waiting for! Go see: www.mylespinkney.com

They rock! They rule! The NOCTURNAL TOMATOES! www.nocturnaltomatoes.com

Sharon Stone was not my only dream girl growing up. Elizabeth Dailey still makes my legs weak. See why: www.egdaily.com

Check out the never-before published poem *Ever Elsbeth,* by Jonathan Martin in Slava Thaler's anthology, *Messages From the Universe.* As with the *Threkjshanelle* series, Messages From the Universe is available through iUniverse.com and other fine book outlets worldwide.

A Mother's Plea

◆

Elisa Kaitlyn Priest is a supercharged assassin fueled by anger and loss in "Funny Little Cigarettes" and "Drop Dead…Gorgeous" by Jonathan Martin. Ms. Lisa Jayne Priest, who portrays her, while not a paid killer, is fueled by the anger and loss of divorce.

To have a marriage fail is in itself, is mentally taxing. I am living proof of such. To have your children psychologically and emotionally abused and being able to do little or nothing about it, is undeniably mind wrenching.

It is said that Colorado is a "woman's state" when it comes to divorce. Plainly, this means that in such a situation, the ex-husband is usually made to suffer financially and has little rights concerning child custody. I myself am somewhat a victim of this unspoken truth.

Sadly, my dear friend Lisa has become an exception to the rule. I am not writing this to "soapbox" or win some election. After seeing to beautiful young kids struggle to show love or illustrate anger constructively, I just felt the need to share this.

Answer me this, why would a father fight so hard to keep his children from seeing a psychologist? Why does a little boy hold so much anger upon returning to his mother? Why does a little girl cling so?

Is not strange how if you have enough money and a sugarcoated tongue, you can get what you want, when you want it?

I ask this not just for Lisa's sake, but also for all the "little ones" everywhere.

Love your children. Even if you no longer love the one who helped make them...

About the Author

◆

Jonathan Martin is just one of thousands of authors to be found within the iUniverse universe. To see the world through the eyes of others, or share your world with the eyes of others, logon to www.iuniverse.com.

The Future is Yours…

0-595-26349-6

Made in the USA
Monee, IL
12 August 2021